Don't Ban Female Education: A Right We Must Uphold

Unlock the Future: The Power of Education for Women"

By

Martina G. Phillips

Table of contents

INTRODUCTION

The power of education for women has been a source of strength and progress in societies around the world. Education empowers women to lead and make decisions that can shape their lives, their families, and their communities. Education can also provide women with the tools necessary to break the cycle of poverty and inequality, allowing them to achieve economic self-sufficiency and social mobility. Education for women can also lead to increased self-esteem, improved health outcomes, and greater political participation. Finally, education can provide women with the opportunity to pursue their dreams and reach their fullest potential. Education for women is a powerful force for positive change and an essential foundation for sustainable development.

Education is a powerful tool that has the potential to shape the lives of women in profound and meaningful ways. It can be used to empower women and provide them with the skills, knowledge and resources to be successful in life. Education provides a platform for women to access the world and to have the opportunity to make their dreams a reality.

Education can provide women with the chance to develop their confidence and self-esteem, enabling them to make informed decisions and become active citizens in their communities. It can also lead to increased economic opportunities, and the ability to pursue careers in fields traditionally dominated by men. Education can also help women to better understand and navigate the challenges they face in their lives, and to develop the resilience and determination to overcome them.

Education can provide women with the tools to challenge the existing gender stereotypes and discrimination they may face. It can help to break down barriers and provide an environment where women can be seen as capable and respected members of society. Education can also provide women with access to better healthcare and improved safety in their homes and communities.

Education also has the potential to empower women to become leaders and advocates for change. By providing women with the skills and knowledge to become active citizens, they can have a stronger voice in decision-making.

Female education is a human right, and it is essential for the advancement of society as a whole. It has been proven that when girls and women are educated, they are more likely to have healthier lives, create stronger economies, and reduce gender inequality. Education can empower women to make informed decisions and take control of their own lives. It can also lead to increased economic growth, since educated women are more likely to enter the workforce and contribute to the growth of their local economies. Women who are educated are also more likely to have a say in political decisions, which can help create a more equitable society.

Education has been proven to be an effective way to reduce poverty, since educated women are more likely to take on leadership roles in their communities, which can lead to better access to resources and improved economic prospects. In addition, education can also reduce gender-based violence, since educated women are more likely to have the confidence to stand up for their rights and to speak out against violence. Finally, providing educational opportunities to girls and women can be a powerful way to combat discrimination, since it can create a more equitable and inclusive society.

For all of these reasons, it is essential that we do not ban female education. Doing so would have serious consequences for both individuals and societies, and could hinder progress towards gender equality. It is therefore important that we continue to prioritize education for girls and women, so that they can reach their full potential and contribute to the growth of their communities.

Females and women are also more likely to raise their children with a better education, which leads to further benefits for society. Female education is key to developing a stronger, more equitable society, and we must ensure that girls and women are given the opportunity to access education and realize their full potential.

CHAPTER ONE: The Benefits of Education for Women

Education is the process of acquiring knowledge, developing skills and cultivating understanding, attitudes, and beliefs. It involves teaching, training, research, and other forms of learning. Education is typically provided by educators, either in formal settings such as schools, or informally, such as through life experience. Education can take place in various forms, including academic, vocational, and technical instruction, as well as through informal activities, such as sports, hobbies, and cultural activities.

Education is a fundamental human right and has an important role to play in promoting gender equality. Education has the potential to empower women and girls and to help them reach their full potential.

The benefits of education for women are many and varied. Education is a key to personal, social and economic development and can help women create a better future for themselves and their families. Educated women are more likely to have better job opportunities, higher incomes and greater access to resources. They are also more likely to have healthier and better educated children.

Education enables women to make informed decisions and to participate in the political process. It helps them to gain greater control over their lives and to make choices that are in their own best interests. Education also increases women's self-confidence and self-esteem, which can empower them to take a more active role in their communities.

Education is also an important tool for women's economic empowerment. An educated woman is more likely to find employment and to earn a living wage. Educated women are also more likely to understand their rights and to know how to access the resources and services available to them.

In addition to the economic benefits, education has the potential to reduce gender-based violence and discrimination.

These are some benefit of woman that are listed below;

1. Improved Job Prospects – Education is the key to unlock higher paying job opportunities and to gain access to more rewarding career paths.

2. Enhanced Critical Thinking Skills – Education helps to develop critical thinking skills which are essential for problem solving and decision making.

3. Better Communication Skills – Education encourages people to develop effective communication skills, which are necessary for success in any industry.

4. Increased Knowledge – Education provides individuals with the knowledge and information needed to make informed decisions.

5. Increased Self-Confidence – Education helps to build self-confidence and self-esteem, enabling individuals to pursue their goals and dreams.

6. Improved Quality of Life – Education leads to improved quality of life, as it provides people with the skills needed to succeed.

7. Increased Social Mobility – Education provides a path to social mobility and can help individuals move up the social ladder.

8. Greater Economic Opportunity – Education can lead to greater economic opportunity and can help people get ahead financially.

9. Improved Health – Education can lead to improved health, as it provides people with the knowledge and skills necessary to make healthy lifestyle choices.

10. Positive Impact on Society – Education has a positive impact on society, as it helps to develop more informed citizens and a more active and engaged community.

There are three types of benefits woman can do for the society

A. Economic Benefits

The economic benefits for women in our society are immense. Women are now playing an increasingly important role in the workforce and are contributing to economic growth and stability. Women bring a unique set of skills, knowledge, and perspectives to the table, which can help to create a more productive and diverse workforce. Women are increasingly becoming more financially independent, which can lead to improved economic security for themselves and their families.

Women represent a large segment of the consumer market, and their economic impact is increasingly being recognized. Women are more likely to invest in their education and career, and this can lead to increased wages and better job opportunities. This can help to reduce poverty and inequality and can lead to increased economic growth.

Women are also making an impact in the business world. They are increasingly starting their own businesses, which can lead to job creation. Women-owned businesses are more likely to reinvest their profits back into their communities, creating more economic opportunities for everyone.

Women are also playing a critical role in the fight against climate change. Women are more likely to engage in green practices, such as using renewable energy, reducing waste, and conserving water. This can help to reduce the amount of greenhouse gasses released into the atmosphere, leading to a healthier planet.

Women are also increasingly taking on leadership roles in the public and private sectors. This can help to create better policies and regulations that support economic growth, reduce poverty, and promote greater gender equality.

In short, the economic benefits for women in our society are numerous and far-reaching. Women are an important part of the economic landscape, and their contributions are invaluable.

B. Social Benefits

Women's social benefits are an important part of modern society. These benefits provide women with the opportunity to develop their skills and capabilities, allowing them to become more self-sufficient, empowered and independent.

Women's social benefits include access to education, healthcare, housing, employment and social protection. Education is key to a woman's empowerment and gives her the opportunity to explore her potential and achieve her goals. Healthcare is essential for a woman's health and wellbeing, and access to quality healthcare services can help her stay healthy and safe. Housing is also essential, providing a secure place to live and work, and providing an environment to support her family. Employment opportunities give women a sense of purpose and self-worth, and allow them to contribute to the economy and their community. Finally, social protection provides a safety net for women who experience poverty and deprivation.

Overall, these social benefits provide women with the resources they need to lead successful and independent lives. They also help to reduce gender-based inequality and create a more equitable society.

Women are socially empowered when their rights to basic needs, such as education, healthcare and housing, are secured. Social benefits for women can help them become more self-sufficient, secure and independent. This in turn can lead to increased economic opportunities, improved health and wellbeing, and greater gender equality.

C. Empowerment Benefits

Empowerment benefits for women in our society are numerous. Women are now empowered to pursue their goals and dreams without the fear of being judged or looked down upon. Empowerment has enabled women to explore and make use of their full capabilities and talents, leading to greater success and realization of their ambitions.

Empowerment has allowed women to break through traditional gender roles and realize their full potential. Women are now able to take part in decision-making processes, challenge existing gender norms and biases, and take on leadership roles in both the public and private sectors. This has opened up a variety of opportunities for women, from career advancement to increased earning potential.

Empowerment has also helped create an atmosphere of acceptance and respect for women. Women are no longer seen as second-class citizens but as equals with the same rights and privileges as men. This has allowed them to make their voices heard in the public sphere and to advocate for the rights of other women.

Empowerment has also enabled women to access education and other resources that can help them develop their skills and abilities. This has allowed them to become more financially independent and to pursue their dreams without relying on men.

Finally, empowerment has allowed women to gain confidence in themselves and their abilities. Women are now more likely to speak up for their rights, stand up for themselves and ask for what they want. This newfound confidence has allowed them to take on a variety of new roles and responsibilities and to realize their full potential.

CHAPTER TWO: Challenges Faced by Women in Education

Women have come a long way in education, but there are still many challenges that need to be overcome. Women are still underrepresented in many areas of academia and face numerous obstacles when attempting to pursue higher education. The following are some of the most common challenges faced by women in education.

One of the main challenges women face in education is a lack of access to educational opportunities. Women often have fewer resources available to them when it comes to pursuing a degree or continuing their education. This can be due to a lack of financial resources or access to quality educational institutions. Additionally, many women may not have the same level of support from family and friends that men have when it comes to pursuing an education.

Additionally, gender stereotypes and bias can also be a challenge. Women often face gender bias in the classroom, as well as in the workplace. This can lead to a lack of confidence and self-esteem, as well as a lack of motivation to continue their education. Women may also encounter discrimination in the form of lower wages or fewer opportunities for advancement.

Finally, balancing work and family life can be a challenge for women in education. Many women are the primary caretakers for their children and must find a way to balance work and family life

There are three types of challenges face by woman in our society

A. Lack of Access to Education

The lack of access to education for women in society is an issue that has been around for centuries, and is still prevalent in many countries around the world. Women are often seen as inferior to men, which can lead to a lack of access to education, especially in developing countries.

In many countries, girls are not encouraged to attend school, due to cultural norms that dictate that girls should stay at home and perform domestic duties, or that education is not a necessity for them. In addition, poverty can often be a barrier to education, as families cannot afford to pay for their children's schooling. In some cases, girls may be forced into marriage at a young age, which can limit their access to education.

The lack of access to education for women has serious implications, both for the individual women and their families, and for society as a whole. Without access to education, women will not be able to obtain the skills necessary to participate in the workforce, and this can lead to a lack of economic opportunity and poverty. Additionally, without access to education, women's voices are not heard, and their opinions and perspectives on issues facing society are not taken into consideration.

It is important to recognize the importance of access to education for women, and to take steps to ensure that they are able to access the education they need. This can include providing scholarships and financial aid grants to allow girls to attend school, and advocating for gender equality in education. Additionally, it is important to raise awareness of the issues surrounding access to education for women, and to encourage girls to pursue their educational goals.

B. Lack of Support

In many societies around the world, women still lack adequate support and are not given the same opportunities as their male counterparts. Women are often paid less than men, even when they do the same job, and are often passed up for promotions and other career advancements. They often face more obstacles in their education and have fewer resources available to them. Women also often have to take on more responsibilities at home, such as raising children and taking care of the family, while their male counterparts are afforded greater freedom.

In some countries, women are not even allowed to drive or leave the house without a male chaperone. This lack of freedom and autonomy further limits their ability to reach their full potential. In addition, many women face discrimination and violence due to their gender. This can include everything from verbal and physical abuse, to sexual assault and harassment.

The lack of support for women in our society is a serious problem that needs to be addressed. Governments, businesses, and individuals must all work together to create a more equitable and supportive environment for women. This can include providing more resources and opportunities, as well as advocating for legislation that protects women's rights. It also includes creating safe spaces for women to express themselves, as well as providing support and guidance to help them reach their goals. By working together, we can create a society where women are respected and supported.

C. Gender discrimination

Gender discrimination against women is an ongoing issue in our society. Women are often faced with discrimination in the workplace, in education, and in many other areas of life. This discrimination is often based on outdated gender roles and stereotypes that have been perpetuated throughout society.

Women are often seen as weaker and less capable than men in the workplace and often receive lower pay than men for the same jobs. In some cases, women may also be denied promotions or other opportunities simply because of their gender. This type of discrimination is illegal under Title VII of the Civil Rights Act of 1964, but unfortunately, it still persists in the workplace.

Women are also often subject to discrimination in education. In some cases, girls may be denied access to certain classes or activities simply because of their gender. Additionally, women are often underrepresented in STEM and other male-dominated fields. This type of discrimination is a major barrier to women's advancement and success in the educational system.

Gender discrimination against women is a major problem in our society and it needs to be addressed. Women should be given the same rights and opportunities as men, regardless of their gender. Education must be made accessible to all genders, and employers must be held accountable for any discrimination that occurs in the workplace. By taking action to end gender discrimination, we can create a more equitable society for everyone.

Discrimination about our women is completely unacceptable in any form and we must take steps to ensure it is eradicated from our society. We must create a society where everyone is treated equally, regardless of gender. We must take action to ensure that everyone is given the same opportunities and rights, regardless of gender. It is important that we recognize the importance of gender equality and work to create a more equitable society for everyone.

CHAPTER THREE: . Strategies to Address These Challenges

A.

1. Increase access to education: Education is a powerful tool that can help empower women and equip them with the skills and knowledge to become successful in their chosen fields. Providing access to education can be done by increasing financial resources, making educational materials more accessible, and providing mentorship and guidance.

2. Promote economic opportunities: Increasing economic opportunities for women can help them gain economic independence and financial security. This can include providing access to small loans, training programs, and job opportunities.

3. Advocate for equal rights: Ensuring that women have equal rights and protections in the workplace, in the home, and in the community is essential in creating a more

equitable society. This can be done by advocating for legislation that promotes women's rights, lobbying for gender equality initiatives, and speaking out against gender-based violence.

4. Support social initiatives: Supporting social initiatives that seek to empower women can help create positive change in our society. This can include supporting programs that provide education and job opportunities, health initiatives that focus on women's health, and initiatives that promote gender equality.

5. Mentor and network: Establishing networks and mentorship programs can help women connect with each other and support each other in their professional and personal lives.

B.Providing support for women in the society in terms of education

Education is one of the most important parts of life, and providing support for women in terms of education is essential for their development and for the development of society as a whole. Women should have access to education and the resources necessary to achieve their educational goals. This includes providing access to quality schools, providing mentorship, and providing financial support.

Schools should be equipped with the necessary resources and materials to allow women to receive a quality education. This includes having teachers that are knowledgeable in the subject matter and providing the necessary tools and materials to help women succeed. Additionally, schools should be safe and free of discrimination so that women can feel comfortable and supported while they pursue their education.

Mentorship is essential in providing support for women in terms of education. Mentors provide guidance and advice that can help women reach their educational goals. They can provide support and encouragement, as well as help with resources and connections.

Financial support is also key in providing support for women in terms of education. Many women are unable to attend college or pursue higher education because of financial constraints. Providing scholarships and grants can help alleviate the financial burden and allow women to pursue their educational goals.

Providing support for women in terms of education is essential for their development and for the development of society as a whole. It is important to provide access to quality schools, mentors, and financial support in order to ensure that women can pursue their educational goals.

C. Address Gender Discrimination

Gender discrimination is a persistent problem in our society. Women are treated unfairly and unequally in various aspects of their lives, including in the workplace, education, and even in the home. Unfortunately, this type of discrimination is often overlooked and unacknowledged, leading to further inequality and oppression of women.

One particular area where gender discrimination is particularly evident is in the area of address. In many societies, women are referred to by words or terms that are not respectful and do not reflect their true identity. For example, women are often referred to as "girls" or "ladies" when they are adults, and often their titles are omitted altogether. This sends a message to women that they are not respected or valued and that their opinions and perspectives are not important.

Additionally, women are often addressed in a manner that implies inferiority. Terms such as "honey" and "sweetie" are often used to address women, while men are addressed in a more formal and respectful manner. This type of address reinforces gender stereotypes and reinforces the idea that women are not as capable or as valuable as men.

Gender discrimination in address also has a significant impact on how women are perceived in society. When women are addressed in a disrespectful and dismissive manner, it sends a message that their contributions are not valued and are not taken seriously. This impacts their confidence and self-esteem and can lead to feelings of inferiority.

The issue of addressing gender discrimination for women is a serious one and needs to be addressed. Women should be addressed in a respectful and dignified way that reflects their true worth and value. This type of respectful address can help to create an environment where women are respected and their voices are heard.

This is often a difficult issue to address, but it is an important one. It is essential that we recognize the impact that addressing gender discrimination can have on women and work towards creating a society that values and respects all people, regardless of gender.

CONCLUSION

The power of education for women is undeniable. Education has proven to be the most effective way to empower women by increasing their capacity to make informed decisions and improve their overall quality of life. Education equips women with the knowledge and skills they need to move forward in life, to become more independent and self-sufficient, to increase their chances of finding employment and to gain recognition in society. Furthermore, education also helps women to gain confidence, develop leadership skills and become more active citizens. Education for women has become even more important in recent years, as it can help to reduce gender inequality and violence against women, improve their access to health care and services, and create more opportunities for economic advancement. Therefore, investing in the education of women is essential for the development of nations, as it creates a more just and equitable society. In short, education for women is the most powerful way to create positive change in society, and should be made available to all women around the world.

Education power is a great force for women, and we must continue to strive for better opportunities for women to reach their full potential. Education is the key to creating a brighter future for all.

Women are the primary driving force behind the development of our world. As we move forward, let us continue to promote the power of education for women, so that they can continue to make valuable contributions to society.

www.ingramcontent.com/pod-product-compliance
Lightning Source LLC
LaVergne TN
LVHW020534160826
845677LV00015B/4047

* 9 7 9 8 3 7 1 0 9 2 3 3 5 *